HALF-OPEN DOOR

T0160141

JAMES FINNEGAN

Half-Open Door

 **EYEWEAR** PUBLISHING

First published in 2018
by Eyewear Publishing Ltd
Suite 333, 19-21 Crawford Street
Marylebone, London W1H 1PJ
United Kingdom

Cover design and typeset by Edwin Smet

Printed in England by TJ International Ltd, Padstow, Cornwall

The right of James Finnegan to be identified as author of
this work has been asserted in accordance with section 77
of the Copyright, Designs and Patents Act 1988
ISBN 978-1-912477-17-3

WWW.EYEWEARPUBLISHING.COM

For Livinia

Dublin-born James Finnegan
has been highly commended in the Patrick Kavanagh
Poetry Competition and shortlisted for Over The Edge
New Writer of the Year. His work has been published in
The Irish Times, *North West Words*, *CYPHERS* and the
anthology *Best New British & Irish Poets 2018*, among others.
Finnegan taught in St Eunan's College Letterkenny and holds
a doctor of philosophy in living educational theory. Married
to Livinia, Finnegan lives in the countryside a few miles
outside Letterkenny in Co. Donegal.

TABLE OF CONTENTS

FOREWORD — 8

OTHERS DANCE OUT — 10

FLOOD — 11

TRINITY — 12

A STONE'S THROW — 13

EARLY-WINTER RUN — 15

NOT TOO SHADOWY — 16

A68 — 17

HOW MUCH DO I CARRY WITH ME — 18

CHOPPING WOOD — 19

HOUNDS AND WHITE HORSES — 20

AN EMAIL TO SHAY — 22

A BICYCLE MADE FOR TWO — 23

ON LAHINCH BEACH — 24

WHEN I WAS GOING ON SEVENTEEN — 25

THE WHITE HAT — 26

INVERIN — 27

THIRSTY — 28

SEARCHING FOR GRIEF — 29

COFFEE SHOP — 30

HALLOWED GROUND — 32

ROOFS — 33

ROAMING — 34

I WAS IN LANESBOROUGH TODAY — 35

ART & CRAFT — 36

THE FEMALE DEER HAVE ANTLERS — 37

LISTOWEL 2016 — 38

CHINESE RESTAURANT — 39

HALF A MAN — 40

ELSIE — 41

I LOVE THE ANIMALS IN ME — 42

DIAMONDBACK MOTH — 44

PENGUIN PARENTS — 45

RED BOAT ON THE BANK — 46

A PRAYER FOR ELSIE — 47

A LIFE NO LESS WORTHY THAN MINE — 48

WHEN I'M GONE — 49

AMERICA TODAY — 51

SYNTAGMA SQUARE — 53

THE MONASTERY OF ST JOHN THE BAPTIST — 54

AU REVOIR MES AMIS — 55

CROSSING A STREET IN MOSUL, NOVEMBER 2016 — 56

EDITH STEIN — 57

YOUR PASTOR FATHER LATER LEAVING DURING THE STORM — 58

PHILOSOPHY OF THE FACE — 59

EMMA MORANO — 60

WHAT ROSALIND FRANKLIN (1920-1958) DOES NOT KNOW IS — 61

STAIRWELLS — 62

ALWAYS ALMOST — 63

WORD — 64

RAYMOND AND ME — 66

SITTING ON THE PATIO — 67

THE MATHEMATICIAN IN ME — 68

FRAGILE KNOWING — 69

IN THE COMPANY OF CZESŁAW MIŁOSZ — 71

ELEGY — 72

A HOMEPLACE SIGNING — 73

INCHOATE — 74

A BLACKBIRD RESCUES ME — 75

THE SPIRIT OF DESOLATION — 76

THE WORDS OF OTHERS — 77

ON GETTING INTO CHARLES WRIGHT'S BYE-AND-BYE — 78

THERE IS A WINTER — 79

HEY DOC WHAT'S UP — 80

SABOTEUR — 81

WOOD AND BONE — 82

EARTH MOVES — 83

CRACKED BLACK PEPPER — 84

THERE YOU CAN'T BLAME THE WATER — 85

NEW MOON — 87

SHOEMAKING — 88

ALL TOLD — 89

COMING TO HIS SENSES — 90

IF WE COULD MEET AGAIN — 91

THE LONG RIVER — 92

NO SUPERFICIAL SHIFT — 93

ROOM WITH FOUR DOORS — 94

ENDNOTES — 95

ACKNOWLEDGEMENTS — 97

FOREWORD

'[H]ow can I not care for the particular' asks James Finnegan in the poem 'The Mathematician In Me' and this question might be the aesthetic fulcrum around which all of his work rotates. An arresting assembly of questions and similes, his poetry has been characterised from the very beginning by this restless quest for explanations: 'there's a complex zebra in me/ who gallops far beyond/ the idea that things are black and white.' Those of us who heard the earliest poems of Finnegan at Listowel Writers' Week and Molly Keane House workshops and readings were convinced from the very beginning that we were in the presence of an important new voice; a cerebral poet, a philosopher, an observer of life's circadian rhythms. Not just the shock of his new materials, the freshness of his observations and viewpoints, but a precision about the alternative weightiness and lightness of words, has been the hallmark of his very distinctive style. As he observes in that sustained simulacrum of 'I love the animals in me' we become a different animal, or simile of an animal, elephant, zebra, monkey, crocodile or eagle, depending upon the poetic task at hand. Poetry can be, ultimately, a safari in the wild reserve of words. Added to his shrewd philosophising is his impressive use of spacing and double-spacing, creating at intervals the opened-out spaces within poems – the 'open field' as Black Mountain poets would call it – where rests and intervals for thought are created. His use of this spacing 'resting' technique is exceptionally brilliant, but it reminds us of the deliberate craftiness behind the making of his best poems; it creates a thrilling advocacy of form and the primacy of form in poetic making. If there is any victimhood in this collection of poems, it is a victimhood inside language, inside that space where art resides. It is his poetry that moves along 'the long river of patience.'

Here too is a poetry of reading and of life observed. Life, as observed, includes a journey downhill to early Mass from Castletown Cross or observations on a winter's evening run or at Lahinch Beach; or chopping wood on a Good Friday or the break-up of The Beatles in April, 1970 – all of these various and variable moments cohering into the biography of our one poet. And, as a counterpoint, we have the absorbed intellectual world as it impinges upon the poems arrived at: Raymond Carver, a crucial and poignant presence in this poetry, or Simon Armitage's *Paper Aeroplane Horses* read in a café, or Paul Muldoon and the poet's lost cat, or Mary Oliver's birds and frogs; or Father Bernard Lonergan's theory of a moving viewpoint that allows James Finnegan to read his way into both Charles Wright and Tomas Tranströmer. Everything is absorbed and nothing is lost as the poet weaves and twists through gale force winds of high literature; the poet surviving what is either read or what is suffered; surviving with enough recollection and élan to complete these beautiful and satisfying poems.

This first collection is the authentic record of a journey well made in life as in verse-craft. The thought can be complex and the poem may be difficult, but for the reader of poetry this is a journey well worth sharing with a marvellous, singular poet.

Thomas McCarthy

OTHERS DANCE OUT

when winds batter me fully open
    to brilliant white light
more than I can take
    I shelter in the shade

on a steel grey day
I push the door to a narrow cut
make myself as welcome as a slit throat
    light enough
    for flickering hope

when I'm a half-open door
    a golden mean
    a fine-tuned balance
others dance out and in

FLOOD

my father and I stride to early mass
downhill from Castletown Cross
past Matthews' old house   its hedge
once hid our sibling gang for half a day
    before our brother Francis left us

past horses   past wire and canvas tents   past clotheslines
past rusted pots with steaming water
all the way to the flooded road
which blocks our short-cut to St Joseph's
I then hear my father say *fuck*

and in an instant
here is a lesser saint
the man who leads me through water

TRINITY

Adam   the dusty horse
      somewhat lost since Eve left
    ignores me   continues to munch the green stubble

    I run on for a few kilometres
a grey cat   two front paws off the ground
    pushes the top of her head
                      into my left palm

              I run on again
a labrador walks towards me
    to be stroked   I oblige
                      neither of us breaking stride

A STONE'S THROW

sitting in my car reading *Slingshot*
by Yusef Komunyakaa
two boys with LS Lowry limbs
walk by with July happiness

laughing & bouncing
a Bucksminster ball
matching black & green rucksacks
the taller wearing blue   the other yellow & black

both with navy-blue gym shoes   rimmed white
& ankle socks   busy spring
 to their summer stride   brothers
   got to be brothers I decide

nineteen degrees   going somewhere
purposeful & probably loved
remind me of Bren   Mike & me
one school day in Dundalk

moons & moons ago
& Pepper the terrorist
who had bullied
each of us singularly

something in us changed
we became a trinity of brothers
on that particular day
Pepper shouted at us 80 metres away

rather than run we held our ground
& threw stones instead
Pepper's head at a corner
more than a stone's throw away

until I was gifted with a David swing
a slick slim piece of slate
shaping a narrative arc
like a negative quadratic

which landed with a delicious clank
on his head   we saw it land
& heard the sound echo the seen
    Pepper ground to a halt

we were mesmerised by the thrilling aim
& laughed & laughed with excited relief
that we had made salt of Pepper
    we never saw him again

EARLY-WINTER RUN

out for a winter's evening run
I stop still by the sound of water
treble sound upstream   bass sound down
my stereo ears take it all in

I run on   lift my hat off
press its soft fleece to my mouth
feel the warmth of breath
        on my face

my uphill stride beats an iambic da-dum
        car tyres hum the tarmac
polyurethane soles ti-tum along the road
no pyrrhic nor spondee stress tonight

the darkness of December descends
        envelops me in a bleak cold cloak
a gibbous moon splits the cloud behind me
        a comforting of sorts

NOT TOO SHADOWY

it's not just a question of ash & bone
there is much more to it than that
    on the first attempt   the hearse breaks down
    on the second   the receiving cuboid
of air floods   on the third   the water
pumped clear   the coffin is lowered
but surfaces in the quiet of final prayer
& floats up through the open grave

the curlews & oystercatchers
& hooded crows etch curves & tracks
in the sky & sands of Lochinver

    of those who wander from care
a local gardener once said
when it gets dark they want to head for home

A68

one might think that A68
is an international paper size
consumed by rare bookish bacteria
    or more likely   a major road
running from Darlington to Edinburgh
      it could also be an iceberg
   about the size of Delaware
     or County Galway
recently calved by the Larsen C
Ice Shelf in the Antarctic winter
         July 2017
   a birthing that takes decades
scientists spent years observing the rift
                  now the attention's on the drift

HOW MUCH DO I CARRY WITH ME

yesterday morning   last week   my wedding day
   the Sunday morning the police called
    to my car-less phone-less home in eighty-six
    to tell me my father died
holding tightly onto a rope
attached to a felucca
whilst swimming in the fast flowing Nile
   walking to the snow-covered summit
   of Petit Mount Blanc a few summers ago
and last May
   the shaded cliff-edge church in Lousios Gorge
   experiencing falling in love like breathing clear air
a deep and wide and hidden story inside
the frontier country of memory
the good dark of the conscious
and unconscious collective
often far beyond image   far beyond language
often an inchoate push or pull
a flashing flight from the ineffable
   what do I carry with me that makes me   me
what is it that leads me to be at rest
   more than endorphins after a run
more than the first shot of caffeine in the day
more than a thirty minute quiet time
more than being loved by someone
     though that helps
    the truly gritty grainy ground of recollection
the inexhaustible mystery of being
vast depths below an anchor drop
heaven-spent heights above the flight of a bird
widths wider than a continent
an inner landscape of constant beckoning –

it is impossible to say how much

CHOPPING WOOD

Billy asks me help him chop some wood
one sunny Good Friday   we pull the full
trailer of logs home at five like we've cut
down the wooden cross of the broken Christ

on the way we joke with joyful banter
stack the fuel at Billy's   more laughter
on a high   trip over words   say goodbyes
which time shadow and scythe solidify

the logs turn eventually to ash
nothing matches the marked memory
cheerful voice and bright endorphin face
casting some life on a torn Friday

HOUNDS AND WHITE HORSES

after Michael Longley

Here are two scenes from the hounds of the sea
lodged in an inner cavern –
a no to the priesthood by my father
after a thirty day retreat,
post-war Kiltegan;
a 1947 yes to being a radio officer
in white uniform with the Marconi Company
telecommunicating ships' news
for the next three years.

All the way to Durban to see separate black
and white queues form for drinking water –
a collared cramp for a colourless liquid:
In Madagascar monkeys threw coconuts
at the crew heading up river
which, laughing, they threw back;
a skeletal sharing of memories here,
apart from a long train journey inland once
made to get to Christmas Mass.

Later, in the midlands, he would scent salt-spray
and whisk the whole family beyond Spiddal
to the sea of his teenage years.
There's a photo of him in sailor whites
in the front garden of his childless uncle and aunt
who brought him and his brother up.

Sometimes, when he visited his big family in Gort,
he was teased with gentle cruelty
to make him feel an outsider
How's the Connemara man?

The hurt would soon pass for
this man who brought me up
with a love of the sea.

AN EMAIL TO SHAY

hello Shay   how are things in heaven

I imagine John Lennon is surprised
and I'd say   it's a human quandary
for Jean Paul Sartre

have you talked to Fran
I bet he is glad to see you
is he still four or is he fifty-seven now

do you miss your Monica
how do you occupy your time
is there time there
is there a there

remember Mr Gunning who gave me
money and a meal for picking potatoes
he rang the cash register   out slid the till
how much do you think it's worth
I said seven shillings and sixpence
and he gave me ten shillings
tell him I am asking for him

by the way
I sometimes wear
your ESB boots
when out cutting the grass
especially when the grass is wet

talk to you soon   your son

A BICYCLE MADE FOR TWO

walking home Tuesday
a tandem passes by me
    father at the front
young son bent low pedalling
    man light-heartedly humming

    father's happy tune
young boy bent low pedalling
    his dad at the front
a tandem passes me by
you and I without a child

ON LAHINCH BEACH

there is a ghost-mirror dull ice-sheet sheen
making a couple ten feet tall
on Lahinch Beach in late July
   will they feel uplifted after their walk

there's a collie-like dog with bushy tail
flying the shoreline with a happy hop
chasing oystercatchers away
   dashes over pebbles boulders banking

onto the road and back to the steps
to join her or his human family
   there is a girl with a long coat bare feet
looking out to sea unaware of being seen

man and three kids   are also stretched
blown along like a daisy chain
   surf boards yellow blue green and white
at rest carried skimming over water

cranky cloud cover evicted from Galway
manages to contain its mood for now
the oystercatchers return to where they were
   I already miss the dog's happy hop

WHEN I WAS GOING ON SEVENTEEN

Elvis was getting it back together
The Beatles were falling apart
our truck trundled north
Eamonn Lowry sang the Boston Burglar
knew all the words but not the tune
stopped at Finner Camp for a bite to eat
moved up-country to Fort Dunree

on that sunny day
we cut along the cliff-edge to the beach
got ticked off   on our return
lay low in the billet
missed the first parade

four days later
the lads went dancing in Buncrana
I was on fire duty and
washing dishes for ninety-seven
they had all spun yarns
about who they were
but sheepishly withdrew at midnight
because of trouble in Derry
August the twelfth nineteen sixty nine

the next day
we were sent home early
a 180 mile trip southward

when my mother saw me
the welcome given
mirrored one
given to a son
returning from war
which is exactly what it turned out to be

THE WHITE HAT

it is easy to find
salt of the earth and
light of the world
by the sea

I also find a floppy white hat
which does not belong
to the couple on the rocks
    the woman with the young girl
tells me it is theirs

an awakening
stirs the youngster
on tentative tracks
towards us
and here's the nanosecond
where I hesitate

        held back by the dark
bleak cut of howling rage
the change brought about by
the collared and the uncollared
the unfrocked and the defrocked

I pass the hat to Livinia
to give to the child
and grieve that I hide
my own share of light and salt

INVERIN

I often think I am drawn to the sea
its push and pull and sound and silence
because of my experience in the womb

but there is something else drawing me to Inverin
where my father Shay lived his teenage years
with a childless aunt and uncle

and from where he left in '47
telecommunicating ships' news
for three years with the Marconi Company

he brought us up with a love of the sea
of spoken Irish and Connemara
but there is something more drawing me to Inverin

Murt and Bibby gave Shay a home in Sailearna
where he had space and comfort and time
to find the good in things

perhaps it is a place where I can feel loved
because I felt loved by my father
but there is more to it than that

something else is drawing me to Inverin

THIRSTY

in April 1970
The Beatles break up
leave me breathless and broken
exhausted would they ever re-unite
Matthew Mark John and Paul
George Ringo Luke and John
more popular than the Gospel man
John and Yoko move to New York

recently on Fuji TV
boyband SMAP apologize
to the Japanese public for 'causing trouble'
with talk about their split
after 25 years
Sports Music Assemble People
are staying together   it seems
Prime Minister Shinzo Abe is glad
because it is what the fans want

in the wasteland after conflict
the ground is dry-boned and dusty
it will never be the same again

at high tide the Ramelton river is wider
the far bank appears further away
no flashing kingfisher today
the crows on bare branches and rooftops
barely move in January light
a lone swan floats on wide water
dips its beak
and unselfconsciously
stretches to the sky
as if quenching a long-necked thirst
leans back curves its neck forward

SEARCHING FOR GRIEF

for Helen Reilly 1924-2015

I kiss
the loss of you
embracing life laughing
Elder Helen leaves the big room
empty

painted
fox and sheep   still
silently wait watching
just above the tick-tocking clock's
joined hands

a dream
flashes through blood
as night unrest awakes
a felt field underground   hello
loved one

COFFEE SHOP

Collins
says prose is the
continuation of
noise and poetry is inter-
rupted

silence
     sitting in a
café I read Simon
Armitage's *Paper Aeroplane*
Horses

which a
cage full of glass
almost blocks there's so much
talk I can't hear what's being said
     I won't

call this
talk prose and chase
the charge this prose is noise
     it's Christmastime in a coffee
cuboid

fitted
with enough glass
to disrupt my reading
     that's all   and this Irish talk sings
the stressed

unstressed
    poetry may
be sound bouncing off glass
where crystal clear hunger hears the
heart's core

HALLOWED GROUND

none
called last night
   another Halloween passes by
   it was the same last year
      a basket-full of coins untouched

grief
called today
   asking me to come outside to play
   I said I must refrain
      she said she'd call again real soon

death
called tonight
   as I was tying my shoelaces
   the scythe swishing through air
      blowing my Tintin hair skew ways

ROOFS

I

There's a low kitchen roof in Dundalk,
off which I parachute-jumped in childhood;
no billow from the four-cornered curtain.

II

Step-down transformer and angle grinder
shaped asbestos roof in Gorey,
one seventies summer before the scare.

III

Kavanagh soared through Reason's roof
after an American kick-start,
his feet grounded in hobnailed boots.

IV

There's a roof through which my friends lower me
onto crowded ground; despite Heaney's and
O'Driscoll's absence, I rise, make my sound.

ROAMING

After reading recently Charles Lamb's
The Superannuated Man
in which he now walks about rather than
to and from

I was pleasurably wandering about Derry City
Monday this week   by the river
taking in the warm sunlight   walking over the peace bridge

feeling the cool peaceful breeze   the surface under my shoes
standing in Ebrington Square   exhaling into calm
open space   looking back over the Foyle   admiring

the sinusoidal wave curvature and slanted masts
of the four year old sail-like pedestrian bridge
        in through the shopping centre   And I chuckled when I saw

Having Problems Roaming?   none at all   as I rambled on
but the humour got to me   I had to stop for a laugh
rang Livinia
couldn't get a signal

I WAS IN LANESBOROUGH TODAY

up Delvin Park cul-de-sac   last pebble-dashed semi
on the left   beside the big field with pitch and putt
and tennis courts and a children's playground   I am
studying mathematics or geography in an upper bedroom
or I'm in some daydream state of waiting   my father drives
up in his long Ford car with lots of electricals in the back
gets out   walks along the driveway in his new tweed suit
tailored by the local tailor with hidden legs   my father tall
with straight back   big chest   my heart lifts in welcome
I was always glad to see him arrive home   unless I was in
a recent bit of bother   all he might say after his *Hello* and
sharing the latest ESB joke might be *I was in Lanesborough today*
it was his way of telling us he had travelled a fair distance that day
      even when I was older he would lay his hand on my forehead
      no words   a Connemara man wishing me a silent good night

ART & CRAFT

invigilating at an Art & Craft event
I'm particularly drawn to an encased green
watering can   probably made of wood
which quenches my thirst as it's shaped like a
cactus plant   one arm straight the other bent

there is also a chair sitting on air
made by a barrister turned woodcarver
    I love the empty space around the chair
& the neat curved shape of the chair itself
    as do the judges who give it a first

there is also a simulacrum of a lost human
    frozen in idleness   facing down and
in   cigarette butts sucking air and light
from a corner of the room   the old man
coughing coughing leaning back & wheezing
    an artist's uncle's later-life portrayed

I fill more time with the green watering
can & the barrister's chair held in air

            now & then I return to the far corner

THE FEMALE DEER HAVE ANTLERS

where does this stillness come from
it's got to be more than a caffeine fix
slow breaths in and out through the nose
the feel of feet in shoes
the smooth cool of page under fingers
heart beating its fifties beat
cold air currents cooling upper jeaned-thighs
    chest slowly rising and lowering
        leather-jacketed elbow on the table
a clear view from a glass coffee-house
    looking out at the outer world
which doesn't seem to be hostile
    nor is it necessarily friendly
bony bottom on the padded chair
left thumb pressing into left temple
two finger-tips on forehead
neglected calves waiting for a walk
    remembered songs on the radio
conversations of other coffee-takers
    once again Charles Wright accompanies me
    blood in full-flow through right fingers
holding the curved-triangular wood
fitted tightly around graphite
as I overcome weak van der Waals forces with ease
                    to give you this

LISTOWEL 2016

at least
the artiste in black
with bushy hair
has another day
when he can choose
to wear a different colour
which happens
to be grey

the racket continues
in the trees

on the ground
the wing-clipped crow
now stilled
legs upward
a young one
shrunken
to the size of a starling

CHINESE RESTAURANT

In Orchid Restaurant, Pembroke Road,
after some wine,
I asked lovely Livinia
what stage her life was at:
a comma, a semicolon, a colon or a full stop?

She said
she felt her life
had come to a full stop.

But it was really a semicolon;
our life goes on.

HALF A MAN

Sundays I usually do something
today I did nothing
watched *Apocalypto* late last night
slept for four or five hours

nine-thirty service this morning
coffee and croissant in Tobin's
counselled a nagging emptiness
over the *Sunday Business Post*

back home I re-read sent emails
to writing groups I withdrew from
back to bed for another hour
up again followed by a forage
for today's and tomorrow's meals

second coffee in a Costa cuboid
read from Frank O'Hara's *Lunch Poems*
though well after four
home to wait for my wife's return

I wrap a pig in a sky-blue cloth
save its charge for a rainy day
the priest's note says *expect it accept it*
work creatively with it
Viktor Frankl speaks of it

at Loch Salt the upper half of a lamb
hangs from a sheep's rear
its head bouncing gently against the soft heather
as the sheep moves downhill
seeks a quieter place to complete the birth
the top part already licked white

ELSIE

after the loss of our cat Elsie
I think of Paul Muldoon's claim
that animals enrich
our humility and humanity

each year for at least two hundred days
I open the door for her
she enters her house
with the grace of a lioness

that slow slinky stretching movement
for eleven and a half years
    I imagine that she brings me to the vet
playing Begley and Cooney in the car

the whiskered vet gives me a sedative
a final goodbye is offered
an anaesthetic is administered
I'm wrapped in copies of today's *Irish Times*

laid to rest in the back garden
a robin visits the next morning
Elsie holds off for awhile
but I'd advise the robin not to linger long

as I look at crows
and take in their now and here
I think of their lifespan
at most twenty years

we don't have a cat or dog or crow
or other animal being to care for now
already   I can't see me   as clearly
as I did   when Elsie was here

I LOVE THE ANIMALS IN ME

there's a frog sitting in my throat
who makes me croak every time I talk
    there's a giraffe in me each time I stretch
for a favoured fruit of the holy spirit
    there's an ageing elephant in me
as I remember your birthday
but forget where we walked last Sunday
    there's a working collie in me
who chases feet sound rhythm and form
and gladly burns in the fire and flow
    there's a serious hyena in me
who quite frankly is fed up
being expected to laugh so much
    there's a young rhinoceros in me
who relishes the charge in life
    there's an ascetic snake in me
    who values the spirituality
of eating one big meal a year
    there's an acrobatic kitten in me
full of independent living
    there's an aping monkey in me
who copies others but not cats
    there's a still crocodile in me
with the patience of stone
    there's an eager eagle in me
who flies the broken wing of life
    there's a wise owl in me
      who doesn't know
    where wisdom comes from
    there's a friendly dolphin in me
with a high view of human nature
    there's a crazy cormorant in me

who plays the stage before big-lensed birders
    there's a busy bee in me
who claims my buzz is bigger than my bite
    there's a complex zebra in me
       who gallops far beyond
the idea that things are black and white
    there's a hooded crow in me
indifferent to my confident stride
               and intake of breath

DIAMONDBACK MOTH

clipping the wings of yellow hair
no slanted word for the slanted one
there's a new kill switch in New York

which self-limits the diamondback moth
    and stops it reaching maturity
as female offspring die early deaths

    genetically modified Adams
controlling the number of Eves
for the sake of cauliflower and cabbage

a bio-rational tactic
for combatting unwanted pests
which can save billions and billions

    as for the cabbage head with yellow hair
    diamondback moths can eat their fill

PENGUIN PARENTS

she loses a THIRD of her bodyweight
he loses HALF of his
she returns from sea
they argue about
EQUALITY

in *REALITY*
she takes the kid
he puts the kettle on

RED BOAT ON THE BANK

a lone heron turns its back on the abandoned boat
lifts and lowers its legs stealthily thro' the waters
    the old boat carries the promise of movement
but fails to translate the river
    dried blood-colour above the waterline
flesh mud-colour below
its stern sunken at full tide

    the upward bow sports
a white capital A metallic structure
balanced on one leg
as if signalling
the boat's indefinite future

    all these things survive
the indifference of a hungry heron

A PRAYER FOR ELSIE

I did not expect you to resurrect
      your claw pushes through the garden corner
out you crawl   bounce the tufted way to me

as far as the weathered York patio
it's Sunday   so there's no surprise
you'd choose today to begin a second life

beautiful   beautiful   beautiful face
a full moon last night   may have wakened you
      it is so good of you to check on me

I am not good right now   I need more time
to take in   you live only one of nine
I ask   that your earth aftermath be blessed

A LIFE NO LESS WORTHY THAN MINE

I guess there's an egg and a hatching
and sunlit fluff and beads of gold
and the tugging sound-thread of its mother
if the tufted duckling wanders too far

I guess there's a danger lurking
as the young one dives and surfaces
with unguarded curves of delight
              and yes
there's the cold eye of a heron nearby

who makes page five of *The Irish Times*
as the young tufted duckling is lifted
    let go   micro-momentarily
floats in air   before being swallowed whole

WHEN I'M GONE

what will it be like when I'm gone
maybe less than thirty conflict zones yearly
which will be a massive improvement
many brains will still be infected with cyberspace
the Amish community will still chop wood
and draw water
from their great grandmothers' and grandfathers' fields
President Michelle Obama will be remembered with love
her husband Barack largely forgotten
Facebook will be a long-faded fad
        as screen-time falters
humans will use their eyes more
the human face will make a comeback
people will blink more often
    in the best order of the best words
cramped post-structuralists and
overly-fragmented post modernists
will dissolve in yesteryear
sentences will become popular again
and will once again make sense
the effort involved
in bringing narrative order
to one's experiential awareness
will again be made with a glad heart
no one will care a hoot
about Paul Muldoon's noticing
of a blackbird chirping outside
whilst delivering his reading
in Listowel
    and in Bellaghy
Seamus Heaney's place of rest will be still
a dander up the road

the political social economic moral sexual
geopolitical and environmental order
                              will be as edgy as ever
some countries will be under water
residents will live in boat villages
above their own homesteads
the italicised Other with capital 'O'
will be as silent as always

there will still be
no way of knowing
for sure
if all we see is all there is
but one thing is certain
I won't be there
I won't be remembered
I will have long disappeared
like sunrises and sunsets
of years and years ago
and it is well known
the sun itself will eventually bow out
and there will be millions and millions of lights
                              to take its place

AMERICA TODAY

I can't say why we landed here
Waltham   eleven miles west of Boston
January 5th 2009
20 inches of snow   ploughs out each morning
    I run with care along Winter Street
and Totten Pond Road to Prospect Hill Park
for a deep-snow jog on trails between trees
by two large abandoned office blocks
    possibly post-crash
then back to the Holiday Inn Express
for morning coffee and a croissant

for the last two nights   eight years later
I have had a dream about an articulated truck
    going off-road in the snow
something to do with fear
        for the future
    my brother Brendan to the rescue
which is funny because he doesn't drive
though he is the kind of guy
you would trust with your life

back to Winter Street   Livinia is with me
    later that first day we drive to Waltham Centre
to see *Gran Torino* by Clint Eastwood
song lyrics by Jamie Cullum

Do you belong
In your skin
Just wondering

all this way to search for calm
acupuncture needles quiver
to the sound of cello music echoing
we visit Impressionists
in Boston's Museum of Fine Art
reconnect with the vibrant
on the way home
call to Barnes & Noble in Burlington
Martin Luther King's *I have a dream*
lifts my breath remembering

mid-January
Captain Chesley Sullenberger
water lands on the Hudson River
all 155 safe
we fly back to Dublin five days later
the day before Barack Obama
is inaugurated to great delight
and the biggest turnout ever

Waltham   today   again covered in snow
and millions and millions of Americans blown adrift

SYNTAGMA SQUARE

a man lies on the pavement in the shade
a cap over his ear to block the breeze
his arm outstretched and palm open
as if the sole metal screw in the clear plastic cup
nails his hand to the ground

on my way to Omonia Square
I pass a motionless man on Stadiou Street
sitting on a step   a carton anchored
to the ground by a stick
on which he leans with his two hands
a still life stirred
no words

further   an old woman mumbles
holds out her cupped hand
again I pass by
    some refugees in sleeping bags
in Omonia Square
caged shut
not much else
returning I once more meet the woman
she is insistent
    this time I give   though not a lot

next day back in Syntagma Square
the plastic cup is gone
in its place two pairs of sunglasses
                        a man in army gear

THE MONASTERY OF ST JOHN THE BAPTIST

— Lousios Gorge, April 2016

in Prodromou Monastery
south of Dimitsana
a bearded man brings me cliff-edge tea
before I climb stairs to the chapel
and further steps up to a small room
where lines of skulls on shelves
don't look at me
one with 1997
in permanent black on the forehead
the not-so-long-ago of it
drawing the cranium's lived life
into the present
and in that
the double-steel cut of
one who was but no longer is
in Mount Athos of the Peloponnese
   in the metal stillness I hear
What I am you will be too
What you are I've been myself
   as I continue along Lousios Gorge
   I wonder
   would John the Baptist
      Prodromou
      The Forerunner
   have something more to add to that

AU REVOIR MES AMIS

i.m. 130 people – Paris, November 13th 2015 (not forgetting the 368 injured)

someone said sadness
is the shadow of a cloud
another   that there is more than sadness here
the sun itself has vanished

you say you are from *Liberté*
that you are *Égalité* years young
and are called *Fraternité*
you also say there is more to you than this litany

there is the space occupied by your body
there is your gift of time
who you are   were   the sound
of your name   your voice   your secret resonances

there are your occupations
pre-occupations   your tastes
coffee   companions   music   sport
pictures of you   and what is visualized

here too   is a bleak present   pressing to an icy past
and the cursed intrusion of an emptied space
memory of you hums a heartfelt mantra
which in cruel cruel time dissipates

your death   seems to be   one
of meaninglessness and nothingness
your life   these things aside   is   was   I hope
something else entirely   something quite extraordinary

CROSSING A STREET IN MOSUL, NOVEMBER 2016

receding hair   grey-bearded   your head bowed
you run towards me with bent back
skimming the ground with your heavy bag
        you make a diagonal cut

across a Mosul Street in Iraq
tan djellaba   dark jacket   sandalled feet
your right hand open   pressing your right flap
        shut against the cold

I do not know if your back is bent with years
or do you bend for cover
from the air strike
as you run from the sun into the hard shade

there are reports of civilians fleeing
to a nearby refugee camp
    your sky-shy locked face frozen
    you borrowed nothing yet your flesh is pounded

are you frightened   are you resigned
are you worn down waiting
are you leaving   how will your face change

EDITH STEIN

for Edith Stein (1891–1942)

Edith rejects an escape plan
by a Dutch official at Westerbork
come   let us go for our people

utter annihilation   in her view   not to go
don't take away my chance to share
the fate of my brothers and sisters

this archaeologist of *empathy*
reaches the little white cottage
    the sound of the Auschwitz train retreating

Viktor Frankl pictures his love
    Primo Levi trades cesium rods
later   one day   Ivan Denisovich

Edith Stein   side-lined by Husserl
and Heidegger   blocked from being
    professor of philosophy

for her   no work to set her free
her habit   with yellow star   on the ground
    naked   she enters   the little white house

YOUR PASTOR FATHER LATER LEAVING DURING THE STORM

the museum
did it trouble you *Vin.sent fan Hoch*
that you were born on March 30th
and that you had a sibling named Vincent
stillborn on March 30th the previous year
   as if you were never a first you
did some pre-natal pre-linguistic rage
lodge in your baby-body throat
when you were surrounded by fluid
and undercurrents along with a current of love

the place
what was it like in Saint-Paul-de-Mausole
did you miss your missing left ear
can *Irises* really feel sad and isolated
did the bed frame and chair in your room
vibrate every time you shouted
or was that your father's voice
   there's an idealized village in *The Starry Night*
under the swirling blues and yellows of the sky
   did you once express in a letter to Theo
a hope that *one lands when one dies*

the play
you   Vincent   a pair of big brown boots
   all others   in bare feet
women lift their heels high and walk
rigid poodles in Paris
   every time you shout
the bed and chair in your room vibrate
   you chase blank canvasses back and forth
across the stage   a sudden loud noise   your face
pushes through   from the other side   bleached white

PHILOSOPHY OF THE FACE

for artist Helene Schjerfbeck (1862–1946)

there is your face your face your face
and ten more faces of Helene Schjerfbeck
in Prince Eugene's old home outside Stockholm
by the sea   the snow   and the trees
February 2013

from Helene young to Helene old
to a sketched skull in '45
like a Scandinavian scream
with arrow eyes and slanted mouth
    a year before the scythe

1939 self-portrait
shows you with a black mouth
one big eye outward   the other in
    head and hair like a Tintin cartoon
you look to my right
I read you better than
if you were looking straight at me

earlier   etched on glass
at the Stutterheim raincoat shop
Scandinavian melancholy at its driest
    another etching that softens me

I sit here looking at a stranger
looking at one of your paintings
probably *The Bakery*
and love the sadness I see in him

EMMA MORANO

(Nov 29th 1899 – Apr 15th 2017)

the sound of jazz riffs and water lapping
the sound of children playing on the beach
the sound of mothers calling their young

I don't have a voice anymore
I don't eat much because I have no teeth
my only child died at seven months

bells ring out the end of the nineteenth
bells ring in the beginning of the twenty-first
    Emma Morano hears them both

works with jute and then as a cook
    her fiancé dies in the First World War
Emma receives an unusual proposal eight years later

marry me or I will kill you
    becomes Giovanni Martunuzzi's bride in twenty-six
    kicks him out in thirty-eight

longevity from two raw eggs each morning
    omelette and chicken in the evening
little fruit and vegetables in later years
    and from having kicked Giovanni out in thirty-eight

    last human survivor of the 1800s
last human good-bye to that century of anxiety
    at some fleeting moment between Good Friday
and Easter Sunday   two thousand and seventeen

WHAT ROSALIND FRANKLIN (1920-1958) DOES NOT KNOW IS

that tall thin hooded crows dance on your name
that Watson-Crick and Wilkins steal your work
that the men get the Nobel
that the woman does not

that your time at Kings would be taut
that you would gain renown for virus structures
that Photo 51 would wing its way into consciousness
    that x-rays would pierce your ovaries

that you would thrive at Birkbeck
that you would die at thirty-seven
that later   in Paris   Mering burns your letters
that tall thin hooded crows still eat food alone

STAIRWELLS

leans on the banister   waits for the mail
falls through the air   no whistle   no sound
                                until the end-stair

was it a jump or a fall   no one knows
though the police   within an hour
                              favour the former

this   a long time after the sale of caesium rods
for cigarettes and food   in one of the camps
                        Primo Levi gone

in another stairwell   Michael Longley and Lucy McDiarmid
smitten by acoustics in late October
                    whistle a Great War song

  birds circle high into the air
but dark clouds still hang in Turin
            long after the war   after the Great one

ALWAYS ALMOST

in the Omani desert   loneliness
the wind has lost its whisper
   no word comes
to take me beyond *always almost*

   in *Apocalyto* Jaguar Paw
breaks the insult-name *Almost*
given him by a cruel captor
in the peaceful hunter's mad dash
and burning rush to his woman
in the deep well   one child in the womb
   the other by her side

no name uttered by another
pushes me down   ever
     and I know
there's the fruitful reticence of St Joseph
but I am not Joseph

   and if I go
beyond *always*   *almost*
   will my desire die
when the sentence is ended

WORD

a rope   a raft
an idea to float

a word is an anchor
a thought to hold
a balloon
inflated stretched
always on the move

a word needs a thinker
a speaker   a writer   a reader
when absorbed it becomes blood
fires the kinaesthetic

face is a word
so is soul
and sold

a word is not a philosophical cramp
it's a trampoline
which bounces meaning
it is a coat
that can be turned
inside out

a word leans against a wall
watches you pass by
often feels forgotten
it is as hard as β-tin
which in extreme cold
changes form
becomes brittle

no Napoleonic button
to shut the wind out today

a word is a rope
which can swing your heart
into that wonder
far beyond anything uttered

RAYMOND AND ME

I have cancelled my subscription
to *The New Yorker* and
The New York Times
the former because I now have a degree
of familiarity with the poems they like
the latter because I don't wish to read
too much about the 45th President

at least there is Collins and Carver
the former not just accessible but hospitable
the latter not just approachable but companionable
    Carver tells me more
about himself than Collins does
      even in a Facebook-free world
                    I would still like that

today I heard about a man called Findlater
who married late
and now has two daughters   and talks about
feeling the pinch of mortality
              I think Ray would like that

SITTING ON THE PATIO

I try not to impose named shapes on clouds
but today I did   *high wispy cirrus*
     writing quill   lying on a blue table

primary wing-feather
next   *the swan   unafraid of heights*
and   *long swimmer's torso   head hidden in blue*

perhaps   *Michael Phelps wind-milling his arms*
     the quill then changes into a boat
floats   *something like two coat hooks*

which on second sight transform into   *an owl*
reminding me of Otus   the Eastern Screech Owl
who like me

stretches wings in evening light
     my words   I hope
not spat out   like an undigested pellet

THE MATHEMATICIAN IN ME

a good eye is needed to distinguish
between russet-brown and olive-green
as they are similar in size   both tiny
the latter with its yellow crown
weighing in at only five grams
        the smallest bird in Ireland
the only one smaller than the wren
    a continental goldcrest
who flew in here to Inch Levels
in late October   and whom we happened to see
on our walk around Inch Lake yesterday

    I'm not that tall myself
after a six-mile run I'm sixty-five kilograms
    thirteen thousand goldcrests
that's how small this creature is
        a life   a lifespan   a heartbeat
        how can I not care for the particular

FRAGILE KNOWING

why get het up
when a sociological poet in a poem claims
their neighbour
who can read the sky
and find the best wild mushrooms   *knew*
that there is no such thing as heaven

    it is with some relief I see
that Mary Oliver   who loves birds
and frogs and ponds and bees and trees
    isn't afraid to write
      I sat down
      on a hillside
      to think about God —

    a worthy pastime

these days it seems
such a sentiment
is not permissible in print

    I have often wondered
how Albert Ellis as an anti-absolutist
in the arena of irrational thought
was absolutely certain
                there is no God

    I also wonder why Richard Dawkins
seems scientistically so sure
    especially when Karl Popper provides
a view of scientific knowledge
which embraces a provisional knowing

on the other side of the other hand
someone who tells me
that Jesus spoke to them recently
scares the *Be Jesus* in me
                              out of me

IN THE COMPANY OF CZESŁAW MIŁOSZ

he accompanies me for coffee in Muscat
brings me into the present
awakens my love for humanity
stirs my desire and poetic intent
helps me believe in
what Ricoeur would call
an affirmative relation to being

you can imagine my change of mood
when I discover I have left
Ches-swaf Meewosh's
Selected and Last Poems 1931–2004
on the return plane in Dublin
   the sudden loss of a close companion
and in that   the loss of a nurtured part of myself
not merely sadness but the metallic cut of grief

though there is something lost
   the best I can do is re-read
in a companionable way
    underline afresh   take notes afresh
and garner support from Philip Larkin's
            afresh afresh afresh

ELEGY

for Helen Reilly 1924-2015

the oak leaves are out   but you have left
I think of you lying quietly
proud chin   lilac beads   in final silence

when will the first sounds break in
who will hear them
will there be enough air should you need it

you moved from   *how are you   I'm here*
to   a full absence
I slowly fathom in the aftermath

how many times I kissed your head
on greeting   and on leaving Esker Road
one of the very few I read poems to

now and then you would suggest a change
and say   *I think you are getting better*
the oak leaves are out   and you have left

A HOMEPLACE SIGNING

in any cave where they take shelter
a line is drawn on the ground by Scott
officers on one side   others on the other

I approach Michael Longley with his book
and a pen   but am held back
by a protector's *'later'*

    I think of Ernest Shackleton
who lost no men and drew no line
    later the protector apologizes

someone on the street tells me
it's quite a dander to where Seamus is
I walk there to see his *walk on air* verse

    after the event in The Helicon
I step onto the platform but am asked
    to step down again

Michael signs my book *with warm wishes*
dates it one x sixteen   I know it's October
but I take it   the x   as a good luck kiss

INCHOATE

it has fallen away
like the last few grains in an egg-timer
    I cannot recapture it
because I did not grasp it
    I can almost see it but not quite
    I know I should have written it down
at the time   and time sped on
there was a 'k' and an 'n'
    could be something like
broken cane   shaken bone
             or
    broken bone   shaken cane
but not these
    and whatever it was
a word with a 'k'
and a word with an 'n'
sparked beautifully when struck
against something
which is totally hidden from me

A BLACKBIRD RESCUES ME

I understand meta-poetic panic
where nothing burns and nothing stirs
   a bleak silence threatening to extend
where one feels the fear of not being
        visited again
   a fleeting fear that never fully takes hold

recently a blackbird visited an open birdhouse
   its black sheen   its yellow ringed eyes
     its yellow-orange bill
a beacon in its bodied blackness
   I observe it for a full ten minutes
at a distance of three metres
the bird's cornered caution with its back to the hedge
as it performs jerky swivels of vigilance
broken only by downward pecks on seed and fat
   multiple reflections in the window
blocking it from seeing me
   my closest and longest encounter
with this beautiful beautiful bird
            all this sensed before I hear it sing

THE SPIRIT OF DESOLATION

I did not expect to be stranded here
I did not expect to lose my way
by the thorn of Christ on a hill in Oman
long after frankincense gold and myrrh
all because I try to please the false god
elected by others to judge my work
      it is time to come back
to the solitude of my own being
   to address
the spirit of desolation within
to cast aside the disheartening
to blunt the blade
of the internal saboteur

today
after reading Miłosz's *Temptation*
I imagine *a significant other* saying
I recognize you

THE WORDS OF OTHERS

Job is asked
which is the way to the home of the light,
and where does darkness live

Heaney writes about being
confirmed by the visitation of the last
and threatened by the elusiveness of the next

Tomas Tranströmer claims that as non-islanders *we gain strength*
not alone from others but *from ourselves*
from the inside that the other can't see
    the vent towards the good dark

and if it's possible to go into this
good dark and express part of it
    is it more than me talking to myself

does *langue* truly dissolve *parole*
and language merely speak itself
where all that matters is
a what without a who

ON GETTING INTO CHARLES WRIGHT'S BYE-AND-BYE

there's a parallel me   walking alongside me
    Bernard Lonergan SJ comes to mind
        about a moving viewpoint   from a moving viewpoint

it allows me   without shame   to be doubly inquisitive
        to slip through the vent
                of Tranströmer's good dark

a kind of grey-light listening
    where I'm happy in the dark
        to acknowledge mystery

one air in   the other air out
    the cool touch of my fingers and palm
                    upon the page
    about a moving object   from a moving object

there is no hello   there is no goodbye
    only the slightest whisper
        of accompaniment

a kind of inchoate promise
        that one is not on one's own
            that the heart might well-beat with purpose

THERE IS A WINTER

there is a winter in falling
    in a dream I fall   a horse is falling too
both of us falling
falling   as is done in dreams

there is a glass floor to break through
to get to the depth charge of change
    no superficial shift but deep structure
the rooted doings & beings of things

I do not know where these dreams come from
    afraid of being crushed by the horse
I manage to land free
    the horse upside down in a trench

there & not there
    in the dream I know it's a dream
yet I fear for the horse
    as I fear for me

in another dream   on a different night
my right hand is missing   I search for it
to store in a freezer & keep it safe
    another hand appears in its place

yet I still miss what's missing
    there is a winter in losing

I fall   the horse falls   a lost hand
two dreams   two nights   there is a winter

HEY DOC WHAT'S UP

after Raymond Carver

yes it seems to be the case and it'll be no surprise
you're not going to die just yet   however we hate
to break this other news to you   we have discovered an outbreak
of extreme ordinariness in your pitiful life
it has probably been there for quite some time
like a stone-still crocodile waiting to lightning-strike
you may have picked it up when reading broadsheets
or possibly from listening to too much late night news on tv

normally   in ordinary ordinariness   we don't say
a word   but yours is a most serious case
so far there's no known treatment for it   we're working on it
we'll give you these   take two five times a day
and always when with others   where you can be seen
and   for now   don't read *The Trial*
this *Rig Lee CG* medication will stop you talking
a good first step to recovery
people will begin to look at you differently
remember don't chew and talk at the same time

and please   under no circumstances   blow bubbles

SABOTEUR

there is someone shouting at me
from the other side of the river
  has been going on for quite a while

  can't make out his words in the wind
I feel like saying to this guy
go fuck yourself but I refrain

  cross the pedestrian bridge
to see exactly what's bugging him

when I get to the other side
he is on the far bank again
still shouting at me

through shafts of sunlight and moody midges
  I can now clearly hear him say
go fuck yourself

WOOD AND BONE

they say that I am
a child's high chair
drawn in to join
a table for two
where one man sits
a man with no child
who would usually avoid
sitting by me

they say that I am
an old man
sitting on a sill
a black shoe half in shade
half in slanted sunlight
face smiling no teeth
crows feet grooved
by strong laughter
long dark coat collar up
the back of one hand pink
the yellow pallor of the other
in soft morning light

they say that I am
a skull sitting on a shelf
in a cliff-edge monastery
looking at no one
1997 blackening
my forehead
a year when
nothing in particular happens

EARTH MOVES

another night of dreams   bell clear
during the night   now entirely forgotten
as the earth moves and rolls its round
through darkness into light
    can the oak tree anchor me
or daisies in retreat or starlings
looking for worms or a full July
canopy of leaves or the white face
of a Friesian calf or clear crisp fuchsia
on a sunny day   as I too move
slowly along the long river of patience

    this morning   there are many things
to think about   in the roll of time
of mother earth   I can't help wondering
    what is the difference   if any
        between the sculpted present
of Günter Grass's *incessant nownownow*
and Tomas Tranströmer's
        Everything else is now, now, now

CRACKED BLACK PEPPER

Major Chance's son got me
        cracked black pepper
I sprinkle it into my sandals
and shoes each morning
            to confuse
the dogs of misfortune

THERE YOU CAN'T BLAME THE WATER

one
the water says I mean you no harm   you drown
the rope says I mean you no good or bad   you hang
on better days the horse pulls your long boat
               along the canal

two
the wind bears you no ill-will
you are blown off a cliff-edge
maybe it couldn't happen to a nicer person
but it did dry your clothes yesterday

three
the snow surrounds you   it is cool
    but not calculating
it did not intend being part of an avalanche

four
the tree on top of you is incapable of empathy
it was just as surprised by the storm as you

five
the mudslide always likes a soft landing
your log cabin – it would be a log cabin
happened to be along its route
    there was no intention to cut off your air

six
the hairdryer in the bathwater
        feels like a cliché
               but
did not intend to shock you

seven
and all those cars
are merely metal on the move

eight
the river bears you no grudge
nor does it remember you

NEW MOON

are the dead behind us
or have they gone ahead

    stone still silence
or we as deaf as they

is the Styx viscous
or will a light raft sink

is darkness solely dark
or is it like a new moon

a black zero of substance

with light on the far side
    where we can talk

SHOEMAKING

you make me something for my feet
    Wellington boots when I'm knocked adrift
in snow   and by the battering ram of life
runners which spring to save my sole
sandals with boats to hold the orthotic
keep me afloat   correct my step
leather shoes which breathe
expansive on the exhale
pores which let micro worries out
and keep macro ones from entering

you also fashion for me hand-stitched slippers
in a morning market in Portugal
the smell of coffee in the air
hill-walking boots
for the weathered ups
and drenched downs
waterproof rubber Rockforts for cycling
and reining in miles
    superlight aeroboard sandals
to keep my feet clean
at pool and beach

I guess
there is
a kind of love
called shoemaking

ALL TOLD

I am told   the earth-womb utters no word
    the island on the edge
comes into being before it is named

        I am told
children become sharpened arrows
parents quivering holds
whom Kahlil Gibran urges to become bows

Isaiah says I have *not* toiled in vain
I have *not* exhausted myself for nothing

        all the while
    I cannot say it
    I cannot say
        can I?
my cause is with the Lord

        I am told
it is not enough to give good counsel
it is not enough to repair and restore

somewhere it is whispered   I must burn inside

COMING TO HIS SENSES

the cry begins
lasts for more than a year
a decent time for a catharsis

his body   by then
can tell how he feels
ready to leave solipsistic selves

hears his name called three times
fully attentive by the third call
a freshening wind billows sails

the world   trees   friends
cats and dogs with short lifespans
push him up and out

a yellow water lily in Sóller
dusted blueberries enroute to Deia
a walk by Cúber dam   all make their presence felt

IF WE COULD MEET AGAIN

before the white hail hits the glass
before the out-held hand tightens its grip
before the rope chokes its own breath
before the narrow slit closes
before *participation mystique* dissolves
multiple and singular selves
before winds slam the soul-door shut
before predetermined intimacy drowns what is said
before cyberspace clouds completely

    if we could meet before all these things
    might I learn to speak afresh

THE LONG RIVER

I move along the long river of patience
      there are few others here
   in fact   none
at least   no one clearly seen
    the sun shines as expected
    on a high alpine meadow
where cow bells boom & insects drum
    & blue & purple flowers play the wind
& marmots stop for a standing chat
        I am in & on the river
& carry a presence over warm green ground
    a marmot brushing against my calf
                                anchors me

NO SUPERFICIAL SHIFT

what does it take to shift a life
from cogito ergo sum
to sum ergo amo
   maybe nothing more
than a good night's sleep
and a good breakfast

ROOM WITH FOUR DOORS

I have no one thing guiding me
there are many things and nothing

there are four doors in this room

The Door (Old Cloister Vaulting)
by Helene Schjerfbeck
                    silent j
golden glow at base and top
narrow line of white on left
      draw me to warm light
the other side of the dark door

      there's a wooden carving of a shepherd *Je suis*
in cream and dark-red robes
long brown hair and beard
      knocking at a door
                asking for help

I have no one thing guiding me
there are many things and nothing

the door to my workplace
made of bright engineered pine
usually open   and when closed
the long clean panel of glass
allows light out and in   and softens sound

      the fourth door is the door
      through which you and I meet
         either of us can shut that
                  any time we choose

ENDNOTES

others dance out – This collection is titled after the poem 'The Half-Finished Heaven' in Tomas Tranströmer, *New Collected Poems*, translated by Robin Fulton (Bloodaxe Books, 1997/2011), page 65.

an email to Shay – 'how are things in heaven' is used within the first line of Siegfried Sassoon's 'To Any Dead Officer': 'Well, how are things in Heaven?, I'd wish you'd say.'

thirsty – written after a studied read of T.S. Eliot's *The Waste Land* (Faber & Faber, 2015).

the female deer have antlers – our local butcher, who is a seasonal deer hunter, let me know that caribou are the only reindeer where the females have antlers; *Caribou* (Farrar, Straus & Giroux, 2014) is a book of poems by Charles Wright.

au revoir mes amis – this poem was awarded a Special Mention in the David Burland Poetry Prize/David Burland Concours de Poésie 2016 English Language Category by Judges Michel François and R Freidman in September 2016 and will appear in an *Ars Poetica Anthology* within the next couple of years.

crossing a street in Mosul, November 2016 – written in response to a photograph in *The Irish Times* (Nov 2016) – thanks to Deirdre Hines for encouraging me to mention this.

philosophy of the face – Helene Schjerfbeck (1862-1946)
was an exceptionally talented Swedish-speaking Finnish
artist who lived in Sweden in her later years.

stairwells – In 'Primo Levi's Last Moments', Diego Gam-
betta challenges the popular suicide-explanation for
Levi's death and is worth a read.

Elegy – Dr Helen Reilly (1924-2015), a GP in Dromore
and Trillick, Co Tyrone, for many years, was/is Livinia's
mother and my mother-in-law. A great character.

the spirit of desolation – Miłosz's poem 'Temptation' – see
Czesław Miłosz: Selected and Last Poems 1931-2004 (Harper
Collins Publishers, FIRST ECCO PAPERBACK EDI-
TION, 2011), page 144.

the words of others – in simple terms, *langue* is objective
language, insofar as that can be regarded as independ-
ent of individuals, and *parole* has to do with individual
utterances.

Hey Doc What's Up – written in response to 'What
the Doctor Said' in Raymond Carver, *All Of Us: The
Collected Poems* (The Harvill Press, 2003), page 289.

there you can't blame the water – written after a slow read
of Nan Shepherd's wonderful book, *The Living Mountain*
(Canongate, 2011).

ACKNOWLEDGEMENTS

Acknowledgements are due to the editors of the following in which a number of these poems first appeared:

The Best New British and Irish Poets 2018 anthology (Eyewear), Hennessy New Irish Writing – *The Irish Times* – Feb 2018, *Canterbury Festival Poet of the Year Anthology 2017, Canterbury Festival Poet of the Year Anthology 2016, Cyphers, Skylight47, Sarasvati, The Bombay Review, Poets Meet Politics 2015, North West Words, CITN 150 – The Poetry Kit*.

My heartfelt thanks to the following for their help and support:

Thomas McCarthy, Jim Bennett, Kevin Higgins, Liam Campbell, Deirdre Hines, North West Words, John Donaghy, Tiffany Atkinson, and FB Friends – Audrey Patterson and Jo Erbacher (Jo Burns).

Thank you to Todd Swift, Chief Editor and Director of Eyewear Publishing Ltd. for saying *yes* to my work. And special thanks also to Todd Swift and Rosanna Hildyard for editing the collection, and Edwin Smet for the book design.

TITLES INCLUDE

EYEWEAR
POETRY

ELSPETH SMITH DANGEROUS CAKES
CALEB KLACES BOTTLED AIR
GEORGE ELLIOTT CLARKE ILLICIT SONNETS
HANS VAN DE WAARSENBURG THE PAST IS NEVER DEAD
BARBARA MARSH TO THE BONEYARD
DON SHARE UNION
SHEILA HILLIER HOTEL MOONMILK
SJ FOWLER THE ROTTWEILER'S GUIDE TO THE DOG OWNER
JEMMA BORG THE ILLUMINATED WORLD
KEIRAN GODDARD FOR THE CHORUS
COLETTE SENSIER SKINLESS
ANDREW SHIELDS THOMAS HARDY LISTENS TO LOUIS ARMSTRONG
JAN OWEN THE OFFHAND ANGEL
A.K. BLAKEMORE HUMBERT SUMMER
SEAN SINGER HONEY & SMOKE
HESTER KNIBBE HUNGERPOTS
MEL PRYOR SMALL NUCLEAR FAMILY
ELSPETH SMITH KEEPING BUSY
TONY CHAN FOUR POINTS FOURTEEN LINES
MARIA APICHELLA PSALMODY
ALICE ANDERSON THE WATERMARK
BEN PARKER THE AMAZING LOST MAN
REBECCA GAYLE HOWELL AMERICAN PURGATORY
MARION MCCREADY MADAME ECOSSE
MARIELA GRIFFOR DECLASSIFIED
MARK YAKICH THE DANGEROUS BOOK OF POETRY FOR PLANES
HASSAN MELEHY A MODEST APOCALYPSE
KATE NOAKES PARIS, STAGE LEFT
U.S. DHUGA THE SIGHT OF A GOOSE GOING BAREFOOT
TERENCE TILLER THE COLLECTED POEMS
MATTHEW STEWART THE KNIVES OF VILLALEJO
PAUL MULDOON SADIE AND THE SADISTS
JENNA CLAKE FORTUNE COOKIE
TARA SKURTU THE AMOEBA GAME
MANDY KAHN GLENN GOULD'S CHAIR
CAL FREEMAN FIGHT SONGS
TIM DOOLEY WEEMOED
MATTHEW PAUL THE EVENING ENTERTAINMENT
NIALL BOURKE DID YOU PUT THE WEASELS OUT?
USHA KISHORE IMMIGRANT
DUSTIN PEARSON MILLENIAL ROOST
LEAH UMANSKY THE BARBAROUS CENTURY
STEVE KRONEN HOMAGE TO MISTRESS OPPENHEIMER
FAISAL MOHYUDDIN THE DISPLACED CHILDREN OF DISPLACED CHILDREN
ALEX HOUEN RING CYCLE
COLIN DARDIS THE X OF Y
JAMES FINNEGAN HALF-OPEN DOOR